Handle Dispute

How Conflict Can Lead to Harmony, Intimacy, and Happiness for Successful Couples

Dr Ashlee Stacie

This Book Belongs To:

____

____

____

Disclaimer

The author of this book, Dr. Ashlee Stacie, is a certified relationship coach and counselor. However, the information and advice in this book are based on her personal and professional experience and research and are not intended to replace or substitute any professional, medical, legal, or other advice. The author does not guarantee the accuracy, completeness, or suitability of the information and advice in this book for every situation or individual. The author is not liable for any damages or losses that may arise from the use or misuse of the information and advice in this book.

The author also expresses her personal opinions, beliefs, and values in this book. These opinions are not intended to offend, harm, or disrespect any person, group, culture, or religion. The author respects the diversity and uniqueness of each individual and couple and encourages the readers to do the same. The author is not responsible for any actions or consequences that may result from following or disagreeing with her opinions.

The author owns the intellectual property rights of this book and its content. No part of this book may be reproduced, copied, distributed, or transmitted in any form or by any means without the prior written permission of the author. Any unauthorized use of this book or its content is a violation of the author's rights and may result in legal action.

TABLE OF CONTENT

Introduction: The Purpose of Conflict

A normal and inevitable component of human interactions is conflict. You won't always agree with your spouse on everything, no matter how much you love and respect them. You will be unique in your wants, expectations, beliefs, interests, and views. In addition, there will be outside obstacles and pressures that might harm your bond. Disagreements, conflicts, and confrontations may result from these disparities and challenges. Disagreement may cause pain, frustration, and discomfort. However, it may also be advantageous, productive, and restorative. Conflict is a sign of a genuine relationship rather than a symptom of a failing one. Instead of being something to be avoided or dreaded, conflict should be welcomed and handled.

Why conflict is inevitable and necessary in every relationship

Because no two individuals are precisely the same, conflict is inevitable. There will always be certain things that set you apart from your spouse, even if you have a lot in common. In addition to being a source of complementarity and attraction, these differences may also give rise to friction and conflict. You could, for instance, have distinct interests, ambitions, habits, values, or pastimes. You could communicate your ideas, convey your feelings, and show your devotion in a variety of ways. In a relationship, you could have distinct roles, duties, or expectations. You can have distinct requirements, preferences, or limitations. These distinctions are just human and typical; they are neither evil nor incorrect. Both you and your partner are part of them.

Because life is unexpected and difficult, conflict is also unavoidable. There may be times when your relationship is secure and peaceful, but there will also be circumstances that might lead to or intensify tension. For instance, in your personal or professional life, you could experience certain adjustments, shifts, or crises. It's possible that you'll experience some strain, tension, or uncertainty. You could have to deal with trauma, bereavement, or loss. It's possible that you'll need to adjust to some new expectations, possibilities, or situations. These circumstances are not pleasant or easy, but they are unavoidable and part of reality. They are part of the experiences that you and your spouse share.

In any relationship, conflict is not only inevitable but also essential. When both parties are involved and invested in the relationship, conflict may be a sign of a strong, dynamic partnership. When both parties are sincere and courteous, conflict may be a means of expressing your uniqueness and originality. In situations where both partners are inquisitive and receptive, conflict may be a way to explore your compatibility and variety. When both parties are open to altering and adapting, conflict may serve as a catalyst for progress and good transformation. In situations where both parties are supportive and modest, conflict may be a tool for learning and development.

How conflict can be used as an opportunity for love and growth

If you approach conflict with the correct attitude and abilities, it might be a chance for love and personal development. You may discover more about your relationship, your spouse, and yourself by having a conflict. It may facilitate improved communication, greater mutual understanding, and quicker problem-solving. It may improve your happiness, deepen your relationship, and boost your closeness. It may support your development as a pair and as individuals. Your relationship may benefit from and be blessed by conflict.

You must approach disagreement with positivity and constructiveness if you want to utilize it as a chance for love and personal development. Conflict must not be seen as a threat or a sign of failure, but rather as a necessary and natural component of your partnership. Instead of seeing disagreement as an excuse to be angry or bitter toward your spouse, you should view it as an opportunity to deepen and strengthen your bond. Conflict should not be avoided or dismissed; rather, it should be seen as a challenge that you can conquer as a team. Conflict should be seen as a conversation to be had with your spouse rather than as a contest to win or lose.

You must also be able to manage conflict in an appropriate and successful manner if you want to utilize it as a chance for love and personal development. To control your emotions and communicate your ideas, you'll need to have some emotional intelligence and communication skills. In order to comprehend your partner's thoughts and emotions, you must possess certain listening and empathy abilities. To reach agreements and compromises, you must possess some problem-solving and negotiating abilities. To apologize and reestablish contact, you'll need certain abilities in mending and reconciliation. To keep your relationship healthy and prevent needless arguments, you must possess certain preventative and maintenance abilities.

You will discover how to resolve conflicts in a constructive and healthy manner by reading this book. You'll discover how to resolve disputes amicably and to use them as springboards for development and love. Through confrontation, you will discover how to attain peace, closeness, and happiness. You'll discover how to become an expert at handling conflict and improve and strengthen your relationship.

How this book will help you fight smart and improve your relationship

Every relationship will always have conflict, but it doesn't have to be harmful. In reality, if you manage disagreements in a tactful and kind manner, it may be a great chance for love and personal development. You will learn how to achieve it in this book.

The most recent findings and recommended methods from the relationship science, communication, and psychology disciplines served as the foundation for this work. It is based on the knowledge and expertise of professionals and happy couples who have mastered the art of transforming conflict into connection. It provides you with useful and tested methods and resources that you may use in your own relationship.

There are five ways that this book can help you argue wisely and strengthen your relationship:

1. It will assist you in understanding the nature and intent of conflict. You'll discover why conflict is an essential and unavoidable element of all relationships and how it may indicate a strong and vibrant alliance. You'll discover the difference between solvable and unsolvable disputes and how to resolve them. You will discover the four antidotes—constructive activities that strengthen

relationships—instead of the four horsemen of the apocalypse, the destructive habits that destroy relationships.

2. It will support the growth of your effective communication abilities and routines. You will get knowledge on how to politely and clearly express your requirements, wants, emotions, and desires. You will gain knowledge on how to actively and sympathetically listen to your spouse in order to comprehend their needs, wants, emotions, and ideas. You will discover constructive ways to communicate your grievances, demands, and hopes by using the X-Y-Z formula, the dreams inside conflict approach, and the gentle start-up technique. You'll discover how to mend and patch things up after a disagreement by using the repair efforts approach, the five apology languages, and the forgiving process.

3. It will assist you in coming up with compromises and solutions that benefit you both. You will discover how to handle solvable issues with the four phases and intractable difficulties with the six steps. You'll discover how to come up with ideas, engage in negotiations, and reach consensus on win-win arrangements that satisfy your requirements and preferences. You will discover how to strike a balance between your closeness and individualism by using the

five-to-one ratio, the 80/20 rule, and the two-oval strategy. You'll discover how to proactively avoid and resolve disputes by using the state-of-the-union meeting, the weekly check-in, and the daily stress-reduction talk.

4. It will support you in deepening your relationship and becoming more intimate. You will discover how to create and preserve your friendship, trust, and respect by using the affection and admiration method, the emotional bank account, and the love maps approach. You will discover how to improve your emotional, physical, and sexual intimacy by using the bids for connection method, the turning toward technique, and the rituals of connection. You will discover how to build and maintain a shared vision, purpose, and values for your relationship by using the four pillars of shared meaning, the four positive viewpoint types, and the magic five hours.

5. It will enable you to appreciate and rejoice in your unique qualities and distinctions. You will learn how to identify and value the special qualities, preferences, and needs that both you and your spouse have by using conflict styles, love languages, and personality tests. You will discover how to recognize and validate your partner's accomplishments, talents, and strengths by using the

celebration list, appreciation list, and gratitude diary. Together, you will discover how to use adventure, fun, and bucket lists to discover and engage in new and interesting experiences.

You will be able to fight wisely and strengthen your bond with your partner if you read and put this book into practice. You'll be able to utilize disagreement as a chance for love and personal development and transform it into a relationship. Through confrontation, you will be able to attain closeness, harmony, and contentment. You'll be able to become an expert at handling disagreements and improve and strengthen your bond.

PART 1: CONFLICT BASICS

Chapter 1: The Nature of Conflict

What is conflict and what causes it

When two or more people have objectives, motivations, or needs that are irreconcilable, there is conflict. Differing views, tastes, values, beliefs, expectations, or interests may give birth to conflict. Pressure, change, or stress are examples of outside variables that may potentially lead to conflict. While conflict is inevitable in every relationship, it is more prevalent and significant in marriage since it involves the sharing of resources, emotions, and a life together.

There is no intrinsic good or evil in conflict. It is an essential and normal component of interpersonal communication. The way that conflict is managed may determine whether it has beneficial or negative consequences. The attitudes and conduct of the parties involved determine whether a conflict is beneficial or harmful.

When individuals utilize disagreement as a chance to develop, learn, and strengthen their relationship, it is known as constructive conflict. The qualities of cooperativeness, openness, respect, and curiosity define constructive conflict. Constructive conflict resolution involves people listening to one another, expressing their wants and emotions, trying to understand one another's viewpoints, and cooperating to develop solutions that meet everyone's requirements. Intimacy, trust, communication, and relationship satisfaction may all be improved by constructive conflict.

When individuals use conflict as a weapon to harm, control, or manipulate one another, it is called destructive conflict. The traits of destructive conflict include disdain, denial, criticism, and obstruction. Destructive conflict is characterized by people who attack one another, repress their needs and emotions, ignore one another's viewpoints, and insist on getting their way. Intimacy, trust, communication, and relationship pleasure may all be negatively impacted by destructive disagreement.

Avoiding destructive conflict and encouraging constructive conflict is the key to resolving it in a married relationship. This calls for understanding, embracing, and adjusting to your differences; cultivating the abilities and routines of successful communication; identifying win-win solutions and compromises; fortifying your relationship and heightening your intimacy; and acknowledging and savoring your uniqueness and commonalities.

You will discover how to do all of these tasks and more in this book. You'll discover constructive and healthy ways to resolve conflicts. You'll discover how to resolve disputes amicably and to use them as springboards for development and love. Through confrontation, you will discover how to attain peace, closeness, and happiness. You'll discover how to become an expert at handling conflict and improve and strengthen your relationship. You'll acquire the skills necessary to overcome any obstacles in your path.

The difference between solvable and perpetual conflicts

Every relationship will always experience conflict, but not all disputes are created equal. While some confrontations are resolved amicably, others are not. Understanding the distinction between disputes that can be resolved and those that are unsolvable will enable you to manage them better and strengthen your bond.

What are solvable conflicts?

Conflicts that can be settled amicably and practically are those that have a well-defined cause and a workable solution. Usually, situational and surface-level problems like housekeeping, money, parenting, or scheduling are the source of solvable disagreements. Resolvable disputes don't stem from underlying differences in personality or ideals, nor do they have a deeper or symbolic significance. Solvable disputes may be resolved by using issue-solving techniques such as problem definition, solution brainstorming, alternative evaluation, and agreement implementation. As long as both sides are prepared to work together and make concessions, resolveable disputes may be sustained.

One example of a problem that may be resolved is deciding how to split up the housework. While one spouse may believe they are contributing enough, the other partner may believe they are going above and beyond what is expected of them. It is possible to resolve this problem by having an open and courteous discussion in which both parties share their needs, wants, and expectations while also listening to one another's viewpoints. They may then collaborate to create a to-do list, designate roles, and decide on a timeline. Additionally, they may periodically assess the plan's effectiveness and make modifications as required.

Perpetual conflicts: what are they?

Perpetual disputes are ones in which there is no obvious cause and no feasible means of reaching a mutually acceptable resolution. Deeper and underlying problems, such as personality, values, beliefs, or objectives, are often the cause of persistent confrontations. Unresolved disputes have a deeper, more symbolic significance and are a reflection of basic demands or disagreements that are vital to a person's identity. Problem-solving techniques cannot resolve ongoing disputes since there is no one correct response or resolution. Conflicts that never end will never be sustained or resolved since they will continually come up again.

One constant source of contention might be about how much time is best spent together or apart. While the other spouse may appreciate intimacy and connection, one partner may value independence and autonomy. Their divergent attachment styles—which are influenced by their formative experiences and relationships—are evident in this disagreement. A polite and impartial discussion will not resolve this dispute since there is no right or wrong amount of time to spend together or apart. The best way to resolve this problem is to have a conversation in which both parties recognize and admit their differences while also making an effort to comprehend and respect one another's needs.

How to handle solvable and perpetual conflicts

Recognizing and treating perennial and solvable problems differently is the key to managing them. Perpetual disagreements need conversation, while solveable conflicts demand problem-solving. While discourse entails investigating and comprehending the problem, problem-solving entails coming up with and putting into practice a solution. While communication focuses on the process, problem-solving concentrates on the result. While discourse seeks to carry on the discussion, problem-solving seeks to put an end to the issue.

In order to resolve disagreements, you must:

- Employ a "soft start-up," in which you strike a kind and encouraging tone to start the discussion and steer clear of criticism, disdain, defensiveness, or obstruction.

- Express your grievance, not your criticism, concentrating on the particular action or circumstance that annoys you rather than criticizing your partner's attitude or character.

- Instead of telling your spouse what they should or must do, make a request, not a demand, outlining what you need or want from them.

- Say "When you do X, in situation Y, I feel Z" when utilizing the X-Y-Z formula instead of "you always" or "you never."

- Actively and empathetically listening involves paying attention to what your partner is saying and demonstrating your concern for and understanding of their viewpoints and emotions.

- To solve issues that can be solved, follow these four stages, where you:

  - Specify the issue and get a consensus on its details.

- o Make a list of choices and brainstorm potential fixes.

- o After weighing your alternatives, decide which is best for you both.

- o Put the solution into practice and assess its efficacy thereafter.

In order to resolve ongoing disputes, you must:

- Employ a "soft start-up," in which you strike a kind and encouraging tone to start the discussion and steer clear of criticism, disdain, defensiveness, or obstruction.

- Don't blame or accuse your spouse of being evil or wrong; instead, state your perspective and the reasoning behind it without passing judgment.

- Don't portray your thoughts or beliefs as reality or the truth; instead, convey your feelings and how the subject impacts you. Express your sentiments, not your facts.

- Employ the dreams inside conflict strategy, which entails delving into the deeper importance and meaning of the matter for both you and your partner and attempting to unearth any hidden goals, dreams, or ideals that may be behind your respective views.

- Actively and empathetically listening involves paying attention to what your partner is saying and demonstrating your concern for and understanding of their viewpoints and emotions.

- To handle enduring issues, follow these six phases, where you:

  - Become a dream investigator and locate the dream that each spot contains.

  - Instead of discounting or rejecting one another's aspirations, let's talk about and embrace them.

  - Calm each other down and ease the tension and anxiety surrounding the matter.

  - Put an end to the deadlock and transition from a rigid, impasse-filled condition to one of flexibility and communication.

  - Make a concession and come to an agreement that benefits you both.

  - Express gratitude to one another for their efforts and readiness to work together to resolve the situation.

It is possible to enhance your relationship and transform conflict into a chance for love and development if you can distinguish between solvable and perpetual issues and use the right techniques and tactics to resolve them.

The four horsemen of the apocalypse: the destructive behaviors that ruin relationships

The four horsemen of the apocalypse: the destructive behaviors that ruin relationships

In every relationship, conflict is unavoidable, but it doesn't have to be harmful. If handled sensibly and with respect, disagreement may really be a great chance for love and personal development. You might destroy your relationship and do irreversible harm, however, if you approach it negatively and hurtfully.

Dr. John Gottman, who has researched hundreds of couples over the course of more than 40 years, is one of the most prominent experts on conflict and relationships. He refers to the four habits he has discovered as the four horsemen of the apocalypse, since they are so fatal to a relationship. Criticism, disdain, denial, and obstruction are these. If these habits continue, they may accurately forecast the termination of a relationship more than 90% of the time. Additionally, they may result in issues with both spouses mental and physical well-being.

This section will explain each of these habits, explain why they are bad, and show you how to replace unhealthy and ineffective communication patterns with good ones.

Criticism

When you criticize your spouse, you are attacking their mentality or character instead of concentrating on a particular action or circumstance that is upsetting you. A complaint or criticism, on the other hand, is focused on certain problems and may be articulated in a positive manner. Criticism is not the same as this. Criticism is a broad and intimate assault that may leave your spouse feeling wounded, defensive, and rejected.

An example of a criticism or grievance might be: "I'm disappointed that you neglected to take out the trash this morning." We decided that you would finish it before heading off to work. This is a sensible and precise statement that talks about circumstances and conduct.

One critique may be, "You're so careless and lazy." You never perform any household chores. You don't give a damn about our family or myself. You make a horrible companion. This is a broad, harsh phrase that disparages the individual and their moral fiber.

Because it may undermine mutual respect and trust, criticism is damaging to relationships. It may also set off a toxic communication loop in which one partner criticizes the other, to which the other reacts with disdain, defensiveness, or obstruction. This may intensify the argument and increase animosity and estrangement.

The best way to respond to criticism is to use a soft start-up, in which you strike up a discussion in a kind and encouraging manner and steer clear of criticism, disdain, defensiveness, or obstruction. Another strategy is to utilize the X-Y-Z formula, which is to say something like "When you do X, in situation Y, I feel Z" rather than "you always" or "you never." By doing this, you can concentrate on the behavior and the circumstance rather than the individual and their character, and you may respectfully and clearly communicate your needs and sentiments.

Contempt

When you treat your spouse with disdain, derision, or mockery, it is called contempt. Of the four horsemen, contempt is the most damaging and is the strongest indicator of divorce. There are several ways to show contempt, including eye-rolling, sarcasm, name-calling, ridiculing, sneering, and insulting. Disrespect demonstrates that you don't esteem or appreciate your spouse and that you have a superior and negative attitude toward them.

A sentence expressing scorn would be, "You're such a jerk." You have no parenting experience. The worst parent there is is you. This is an insulting and cruel remark that expresses disdain and contempt.

Because it may make your spouse feel hated, unworthy, and hopeless, contempt is bad. It may also create a poisonous atmosphere in your relationship, making both of you feel uneasy, anxious, and miserable. Your immune system might be weakened and your stress level raised by contempt, which can have negative effects on your physical and mental well-being.

Creating an environment of gratitude and respect in your relationship is the antidote to disdain, and there are many strategies to do this. To establish and preserve your friendship, trust, and respect, you may make use of the affection and admiration system, the emotional bank account, and the love map approach. Additionally, you and your spouse may utilize the thankfulness diary, appreciation list, and celebration list to recognize and validate each other's accomplishments, talents, and contributions. In order to mend and make amends after a disagreement, you may also use the repair efforts approach, the five apology languages, and the forgiving process.

Defensiveness

When you reject, place blame, or provide an explanation in response to your partner's criticism or complaint, you are being defensive. Although it is a normal and acceptable reaction when one feels attacked or accused, being defensive is neither constructive nor beneficial. Being defensive might keep you from accepting accountability for your deeds, hearing out your spouse, or coming up with a workable solution.

A defensive response may be something like, "It's not my fault that I forgot our anniversary." You are aware of my workload at work. You bug me about something all the time. How come you don't value the work I do for you? This is a counterattacking, defensive remark that transfers the blame and evades responsibility.

Being defensive is bad because it might intensify the argument and increase annoyance and animosity. It may also keep you and your spouse from moving beyond the problem and finding a solution. Being defensive may lead to feelings of guilt, humiliation, or rage, which can be detrimental to both your relationship and your sense of self-worth.

Accepting responsibility for your role in the disagreement, as well as listening to and empathizing with your spouse, are the antidotes to defensiveness. You may demonstrate your concern and understanding for your partner's emotions and viewpoints by actively listening to what they have to say. Another option is to adopt the I-statements approach, which involves expressing your wants and emotions in a nonjudgmental and nonblaming manner. To strike a balance between your uniqueness and your closeness, you may also use the five-to-one ratio, the 80/20 rule, and the two-oval strategy.

Stonewalling

When you emotionally shut down and distance yourself from the discourse, it's called stonewalling. Stonewalling may manifest in several ways, including blank stares, one-word responses, or physical distancing. Usually, feeling overwhelmed, swamped, or despondent leads to stonewalling. Stonewalling is an escape or avoidance tactic; it is not a means of resolving the problem.

Stonewalling may look like this, for instance: "I don't want to talk about it." Please just leave me alone. Move on. This statement exhibits detachment and stonewalling; it is chilly and aloof.

Because it may put a wall between you and your relationship and lead you to feel alone, rejected, and uncared for, stonewalling is bad. Additionally, it may cause your spouse to feel desperate, irate, and irritated. Additionally, stonewalling may make it difficult for you and your spouse to connect, communicate, and comprehend one another. In addition to having an adverse effect on your mental and physical well-being, stonewalling may lower your immune system and raise blood pressure and heart rate.

Stonewalling may be countered by taking a pause, practicing self-soothing, and returning to the discussion when you're relaxed and ready. One strategy you may try is the "time-out," in which you both decide to put the topic on hold for a little and then resume it at a later time. Another option is the self-soothing approach, which involves engaging in a relaxing activity that reduces stress, such as breathing, meditation, or music listening. Additionally, you may avoid and resolve issues proactively by holding daily stress-relieving conversations, weekly check-ins, and state-of-the-union meetings.

Chapter 2: The Styles of Conflict

The three types of conflict styles: avoidant, volatile, and validating

The three types of conflict styles: avoidant, volatile, and validating

Every relationship will always experience conflict, but not all problems are resolved in the same manner. Depending on their requirements, preferences, and personalities, couples manage and resolve their problems in various ways. These communication, emotional, and interpersonal patterns might affect how they connect to one another.

Dr. John Gottman is a very important researcher on conflict and relationships, having spent more than 40 years studying thousands of couples. He has distinguished between one dysfunctional style—labeled Hostile—and three functional styles—labeled Avoidant, Validating, and Volatile—of conflict management in romantic relationships. The work of Harold Raush, who distinguished between happy and unhappy married couples by analyzing partner interactions, served as the foundation for these styles.

Depending on how they are used and balanced, any of these approaches may result in successful or unsuccessful results. They each have advantages and disadvantages. You will discover the definition, operation, benefits, and drawbacks of each of these styles in this section.

Avoidant

Avoidant couples try to minimize or stay away from disagreements. Instead of addressing or downplaying their differences and arguments, they often concentrate on their points of agreement and common ground. They seek to maintain harmony and tranquility in their relationship and seldom confront or question one another. They respect autonomy and independence, and they have distinct interests and limits. They speak in a cool, collected manner and don't show any emotion in their interactions.

Respecting and appreciating each other's originality and variety, as well as maintaining a low level of stress and tension in their relationship, may be beneficial for avoidant couples. In addition, they may maintain their relationship and mutual respect by averting pointless disputes and altercations.

On the other hand, avoidant couples may also experience a lack of closeness and connection, as well as neglect or repression of their needs and emotions. Additionally, they may pass up chances to strengthen and deepen their connection, as well as to learn from and develop from their disagreements.

In order to enhance the effectiveness of their style, avoidant couples must:

- Give them more space to communicate their wants and emotions, and do it in a kind and helpful manner.

- Show more interest in their partner's wants and emotions, and listen to them with compassion and understanding.

- Be more accommodating and ready to talk about and settle their differences, as well as come to agreements and concessions that benefit them both.

- Boost their emotional, physical, and sexual closeness while communicating in a more upbeat and loving manner.

Volatile

Emotional and passionate, volatile partnerships are. In addition to freely and aggressively expressing their thoughts and beliefs, they often get into heated arguments. In order to liven up their conversations, they like to argue and debate and add comedy and sarcasm. Their values are quite similar and interdependent, and they place a high value on honesty and connection. Their speech is bright and active, and they exhibit a high degree of emotional expressiveness.

It is beneficial for volatile couples to communicate their wants and emotions in a straightforward and direct manner, as well as to maintain a high level of energy and stimulation in their relationship. Along with building a common goal and vision for their relationship, they may also deepen their closeness and trust.

But highly stressed and conflicted relationships, as well as harming or offending one another via words or deeds, may also be problems for volatile couples. Along with losing sight of their respect and common ground, they may also intensify their arguments and foster more animosity and estrangement.

Fierce couples must do the following to improve the effectiveness of their style:

- Steer clear of criticism, disdain, defensiveness, and stonewalling, and communicate with more grace and politeness.

- Give your spouse greater understanding, validation, and support for their needs and emotions.

- Find ways to balance their closeness and uniqueness while being more helpful and accommodating when reaching agreements.

- Improve their communication skills by being more upbeat and kind, and deepen their physical, emotional, and sexual closeness.

Validating

Confirming that relationships are composed and logical. They typically communicate their wants and emotions in a direct and helpful manner, and they engage in courteous, mild disagreements. They look for answers and compromises that please them both while also trying to understand and accept one another's viewpoints. Their interests and objectives strike a balance between independence and interdependence, and they place a high value on stability and harmony. They communicate in a kind and upbeat manner while displaying some emotional expression.

Low levels of stress and conflict in a relationship, as well as respectful and efficient communication of needs and emotions, are beneficial for validating couples. They may also attain harmony and happiness in their relationship by deepening their connection and becoming more intimate.

Validating couples, however, may also suffer from a lack of passion and stimulation in their relationship, as well as from repressing or ignoring their wants and emotions. Additionally, they may pass up chances to strengthen and deepen their connection, as well as to learn from and develop from their disagreements.

In order to enhance the efficacy of their style, validating spouses must:

- Give them more space to communicate their wants and emotions, and do it in a kind and helpful manner.

- Show more interest in their partner's wants and emotions, and listen to them with compassion and understanding.

- Be more accommodating and ready to talk about and settle their differences, as well as come to agreements and concessions that benefit them both.

- Boost their emotional, physical, and sexual closeness while communicating in a more upbeat and loving manner.

You may enhance your communication and connection by being aware of and comprehending the conflict styles that you and your spouse have. Additionally, you may balance your styles, gain knowledge from one another, and benefit from them.

The pros and cons of each style and how to balance them

The three functional forms of conflict management in couple relationships—Volatile, Avoidant, and Validating—as well as the one dysfunctional style—Hostile—were covered in the preceding section. Dr. John Gottman, who has examined hundreds of couples for more than 40 years, is the source of these styles.

Depending on how they are used and balanced, any of these approaches may result in successful or unsuccessful results. They each have advantages and disadvantages. You will discover more about the benefits and drawbacks of each type in this section, along with strategies for striking a balance between them in your partnership.

Avoidant

Avoidant couples try to minimize or stay away from disagreements. Instead of addressing or downplaying their differences and arguments, they often concentrate on their points of agreement and common ground. They seek to maintain harmony and tranquility in their relationship and seldom confront or question one another. They respect autonomy and independence, and they have distinct interests and limits. They speak in a cool, collected manner and don't show any emotion in their interactions.

Among the avoidant style's benefits are:

- It may prevent pointless or little disagreements, which can lower stress and save time.

- It is able to value and embrace one another's uniqueness and variety.

- It may prevent disdain and criticism, which can help to maintain friendship and respect.

The avoidant style's drawbacks include:

- It might lead to a lack of closeness and connection by sidestepping serious or emotionally charged topics.

- It may do this by refusing to communicate or express its wants and emotions.

- Avoiding exploration or resolution might cause it to miss out on learning and development possibilities.

In order to counteract the avoidant style, you must:

- Increase the transparency and honesty of your wants and emotions, and communicate them in a productive and kind manner.

- Pay more attention to your partner's wants and emotions, and listen to them with compassion and empathy.

- Increase your willingness and adaptability to confront and settle disagreements, as well as to come to agreements and concessions that benefit you both.

- Boost your emotional, physical, and sexual closeness while communicating in a more upbeat and loving manner.

Volatile

Couples who are erratic are very passionate and emotional. They freely and forcefully express their thoughts and emotions, and they often get into heated arguments. They like to argue and debate, and they like to add comedy and sarcasm to their conversations. Their interests and aspirations are highly overlapping and interdependent, and they place a high value on honesty and connection. They communicate in a bright and enthusiastic manner and are very expressive about their emotions.

Advantages of the volatile style include:

- By getting into intense and emotional arguments, it may excite and stimulate others.

- It may freely and passionately convey wants and sentiments in a straightforward and unambiguous manner.

- Through an emotional connection and a shared goal and purpose, it may improve intimacy and trust.

The volatile style's drawbacks include:

- By heightening arguments and disputes, it may lead to tension and conflict.

- By employing harsh or rude words or behaviors, it might cause each other pain or offense.

- By concentrating on conflicts and differences, it might lose sight of common ground and respect.

To counterbalance the erratic style, you must:

- When communicating, practice more decency and civility and refrain from being critical, disrespectful, defensive, or obstructionist.

- Increase your empathy for and support for your partner's needs and emotions by confirming and validating them.

- When coming to agreements and compromises, be more cooperative and adaptable, and strike a balance between your closeness and uniqueness.

- Boost your emotional, physical, and sexual closeness while communicating in a more upbeat and loving manner.

Validating

Affirming that peaceful and sensible relationships exist. Their confrontations are usually courteous and mild, and they communicate their demands and emotions in a manner that is both clear and productive. They look for concessions and answers that work for them both, while also trying to understand and accept one another's points of view. They have a balance between independence and dependency in their interests and ambitions, and they place a high value on stability and harmony. They communicate in a kind and upbeat manner and are quite emotionally expressive.

Benefits of the validating style include:

- By handling disagreements civilly and calmly, it may lessen tension and hostility.

- It may convey wants and sentiments in a straightforward, constructive manner, successfully and politely communicating them.

- By acknowledging and valuing one another's viewpoints, it may deepen relationships and foster closeness.

- By figuring out concessions and solutions that work for both of them, it may bring about peace and contentment.

Among the validating style's drawbacks are:

- Conflicts that are predictable and modest might lead to a lack of enthusiasm and stimulation.

- By conceding too often or too rapidly, it might stifle or ignore emotions and desires.

- By settling for acceptable concessions or solutions, it may miss out on chances to develop and learn.

The validating style must be balanced by:

- Be more forthright and honest about your wants and emotions, and communicate them in a kind and helpful manner.

- Increase your level of curiosity, pay closer attention to your partner's wants and emotions, and listen to them with compassion and understanding.

- Find solutions and compromises that benefit both of you by being more open-minded and accommodating while handling and resolving problems.

- Enhance your emotional, physical, and sexual closeness by communicating in a more positive and loving manner.

The importance of emotional intelligence and communication skills in conflict resolution

The importance of emotional intelligence and communication skills in conflict resolution

Your emotional intelligence (EI) is one of the most significant characteristics that determines how you manage conflict. Empathy is the capacity to recognize, comprehend, and control your own feelings as well as those of others. By improving your understanding, empathy, and communication, Emotional Intelligence may assist you in effectively resolving problems. Emotional intelligence (EI) may also assist you in controlling your emotions, listening to your spouse, and communicating clearly.

Your communication abilities have a significant role in how you manage conflict. The capacity to properly and clearly transmit and receive information is known as communication skills. Effective conflict resolution may be achieved via the use of communication skills, which enhance listening, articulation, and problem-solving abilities. Additionally, having good communication skills may help you resolve conflicts, define expectations, and prevent misunderstandings.

This part will teach you more about the role that emotional intelligence (EI) and communication skills play in resolving conflicts, as well as how to utilize and improve them in your relationship.

How EI and communication skills can help you resolve conflicts

Conflict resolution may be facilitated by EI and effective communication in a number of ways, including:

- They may assist you in identifying and controlling your own feelings so that you don't respond rashly or violently. For instance, you may use emotional intelligence (EI) to calm down and utilize communication skills to express your thoughts in a healthy manner rather than lashing out or shutting down if your partner's words or actions have hurt or angered you.

- They may assist you in understanding and sharing your partner's feelings without passing judgment or brushing them off. For instance, you may use emotional intelligence (EI) to detect your partner's feelings of sadness or anxiety and communication skills to listen to them with empathy and support instead of downplaying or condemning them.

- They can assist you in politely and clearly expressing your wants and emotions without placing blame or accusations on your spouse. For instance, instead of assuming or making demands, you may use emotional intelligence (EI) to recognize your needs and emotions and utilize communication skills to communicate them in a non-judgmental and non-blaming manner if you're dissatisfied or disappointed by your partner's actions or choices.

- They may assist you in actively and sympathetically listening to your partner's wants and emotions without interrupting or disputing them. Instead of defending or justifying yourself, you may use emotional intelligence (EI) to pay attention to your partner's feelings and utilize your communication skills to listen to them with interest and understanding if they are upset or hurt by your words or actions.

- They can assist you in avoiding being obstinate or giving up on your own demands and instead help you come to compromises and solutions that benefit you both. To discuss, negotiate, and come to an agreement on a win-win solution that satisfies both of your wants and preferences, for instance, you might utilize Emotional Intelligence (EI) to respect and value your differences in opinion and preference from your spouse.

You may strengthen your relationship and use conflict as a chance for love and personal development by using EI and communication techniques in conflict resolution. Conflict may lead to peace, closeness, and enjoyment. You may improve and strengthen your relationship by learning how to handle disagreements.

How to develop and use EI and communication skills in conflict resolution

It takes time and work to develop and use Emotional Intelligence (EI) and communication skills for conflict resolution, but it is an investment worth making in your personal and professional relationships. Here are some pointers and techniques to assist you in cultivating and using your communication and emotional intelligence in dispute resolution:

- In order to improve your EI, you can:

  - Develop self-awareness by keeping an eye on your own feelings, thoughts, and behaviors, as well as how they impact you and other people.

  - Develop self-regulation skills by choosing constructive and positive reactions while maintaining control over your own feelings, ideas, and behaviors.

- Engage in self-motivation by using your own feelings, ideas, and behaviors to drive yourself toward your objectives and get beyond obstacles.

  - Develop your social awareness by seeing and comprehending the feelings, ideas, and behaviors of others, as well as how they impact you and other people.

  - Develop your social skills by using your own feelings, ideas, and behaviors to communicate and connect with others in a polite and productive way.

- To improve your ability to communicate, you can:

  - Engage in active listening by paying attention to what the other person is saying, demonstrating your understanding of their viewpoints, and demonstrating your concern for them.

  - Aim for assertive communication, which means communicating your wants and emotions in a courteous and unambiguous manner. Avoid using passive, aggressive, or passive-aggressive communication styles.

- Give and accept positive and negative feedback in a useful and courteous manner by practicing constructive feedback, and steer clear of praise or criticism.

  - Engage in problem-solving exercises where you and the other person collaborate to identify the issue, generate potential solutions, assess alternatives, and carry out agreements.

  - Engage in conflict resolution by using the abilities and tactics outlined above to resolve disputes in a constructive and efficient manner.

- You may use your communication and emotional intelligence to resolve disputes by:

  - Employ a "soft start-up," in which you strike a kind and encouraging tone to start the discussion and steer clear of criticism, disdain, defensiveness, or obstruction.

  - Say "When you do X, in situation Y, I feel Z" when utilizing the X-Y-Z formula instead of "you always" or "you never."

- o Employ the dreams inside conflict strategy, which entails delving into the deeper importance and meaning of the matter for both you and your partner and attempting to unearth any hidden goals, dreams, or ideals that may be behind your respective views.

- o To solve issues that can be solved, follow these four stages, where you:

  - Specify the issue and get a consensus on its details.

  - Make a list of choices and brainstorm potential fixes.

  - After weighing your alternatives, decide which is best for you both.

  - Put the solution into practice and assess its efficacy thereafter.

- o To handle enduring issues, follow these six phases, where you:

  - Become a dream investigator and locate the dream that each spot contains.

- Instead of discounting or rejecting one another's aspirations, let's talk about and embrace them.

- Calm each other down and ease the tension and anxiety surrounding the matter.

- Put an end to the deadlock and transition from a rigid, impasse-filled condition to one of flexibility and communication.

- Make a concession and come to an agreement that benefits you both.

- Express gratitude to one another for their efforts and readiness to work together to resolve the situation.

Chapter 3: The Topics of Conflict

The common topics that couples fight about, such as money, sex, parenting, chores, etc.

This section explains the most frequent arguments between couples, why they are so troublesome, and practical solutions for handling them.

Money

For good reason, it's often believed that arguments over money are the most frequent source of contention in relationships. Numerous concepts, including power, security, independence, prestige, and pleasure, may be represented by money. Additionally, distinct objectives, tastes, routines, or expectations might be reflected in the money. When a couple's salaries, debts, spending, saving, or investment habits diverge, money may lead to arguments. When a couple needs to make financial choices together, including planning, budgeting, or shopping, money may also lead to arguments.

To resolve financial disputes, you must:

- Avoid lying or withholding information about your financial status; instead, be upfront and honest about your objectives, worries, and state of mind.

- Recognize and respect one another's financial personalities, needs, and values; do not pass judgment on or provide criticism on one another's financial decisions.

- Establish and adhere to a reasonable, shared budget, and set aside a certain amount of money for each partner's own use.

- If you are experiencing severe financial issues, such as debt, bankruptcy, or fraud, get expert assistance.

Sex

Another frequent source of contention for couples, particularly those in committed partnerships, is sex. Numerous concepts, including love, closeness, pleasure, and fulfillment, may be represented via sex. Diverse imaginations, expectations, tastes, and wants may also be reflected in sexual behavior. When partners vary in their degrees of sexual desire, frequency, or quality, it may lead to conflict. When partners must handle sexual problems like adultery, dysfunction, or unhappiness, sex may also lead to arguments.

In order to resolve sexual disputes, you must:

- Instead of placing blame or shame on one another for sexual issues, be open and honest in your communication about your needs, preferences, and emotions.

- Recognize and respect each other's limits, preferences, and sexual differences; do not coerce or compel one another into having sex.

- Establish and maintain a lighthearted and upbeat sexual environment, and try out novel approaches to spice up your relationship.

- If you suffer from severe sexual issues, such as abuse, addiction, or trauma, get expert assistance.

Parenting

For couples who already have children or want to have children, parenting is another frequent source of contention. Numerous concepts, like legacy, care, and duty, may be associated with parenting. Various parenting philosophies, approaches, or standards may also be seen in parenting. Differing opinions on how to punish, educate, and nurture children may lead to arguments between spouses throughout the parenting process. When a couple juggles their duties as parents and a relationship, parenting may sometimes lead to conflict.

To resolve disputes as a parent, you must:

- When discussing your parenting beliefs, objectives, and worries with your kids, be open and truthful with each other. Don't undermine or contradict one another in front of the kids.

- Recognize and value one another's parenting approaches, as well as your own and your children's, and refrain from comparing or competing with one another.

- Establish a parenting schedule that is both mutually acceptable and consistent, and divide up the responsibilities and choices evenly.

- If you are experiencing severe parenting issues, like abuse, neglect, or divorce, get expert assistance.

Chores

Another frequent source of contention for cohabiting couples is domestic chores. Numerous concepts may be represented by chores, including effort, order, and cleanliness. Different routines, expectations, or standards may also be reflected in chores. When two people are not as involved, contributing, or satisfied with the domestic chores, it might lead to conflict. Couples who must split, assign, or discuss domestic duties may also experience conflict as a result of housework.

To resolve disputes about duties, you must:

- Avoid nagging or whining about the duties; instead, be open and honest in your communication about your requirements, preferences, and concerns about your home.

- Recognize and respect one another's expectations, norms, and domestic practices; do not dictate or criticize one another's task assignments.

- Establish and adhere to a just and mutually agreed-upon home plan, and give each spouse specific tasks and timetables.

- If you are dealing with significant issues in your home, such as clutter, hoarding, or filth, get expert assistance.

The underlying issues and needs behind each topic

You read about the most frequent causes of conflict in marriages in the previous section, including finances, sex, parenting, and housework. This part will teach you more about the demands and underlying problems that each subject has, as well as how to solve them in a constructive and efficient manner.

Money

For good reason, it's often believed that arguments over money are the most frequent source of contention in relationships. Numerous concepts, including power, security, independence, prestige, and pleasure, may be represented by money. Additionally, distinct objectives, tastes, routines, or expectations might be reflected in the money. When a couple's salaries, debts, spending, saving, or investment habits diverge, money may lead to arguments. When a couple needs to make financial choices together, including planning, budgeting, or shopping, money may also lead to arguments.

Money disputes often stem from underlying difficulties and desires that are connected to:

- Control: When money is limited or unpredictable, it may either offer one a feeling of control or a lack of control over their life and decisions. In relationships, money may sometimes lead to power struggles or dependence, particularly when one spouse handles the household finances or makes more money than the other. Couples may argue over how to balance their individual and shared interests or who should have the last say when it comes to financial matters.

- Security: When money is scarce or uncertain, it may either give one a feeling of insecurity and instability or a lack thereof. One's lifestyle and level of living may also be impacted by money, particularly in situations where income or costs fluctuate or provide difficulties. Divorces may arise from disagreements over how to handle financial stress or uncertainty, as well as how much and how to save.

- Freedom: When money is scarce or constrained, it may provide both a feeling of freedom and opportunity, or neither. Dreams and objectives may also be facilitated or hindered by money, particularly if they diverge or are irreconcilable between couples. Couples may argue over how to balance their independence and commitment or how to follow or support each other's personal or professional goals.

In order to resolve the fundamental demands and problems that underlie financial disputes, you must:

- Avoid lying or withholding information about your financial status; instead, be upfront and honest about your objectives, worries, and state of mind.

- Recognize and respect one another's financial personalities, needs, and values; do not pass judgment on or provide criticism on one another's financial decisions.

- Establish and adhere to a reasonable, shared budget, and set aside a certain amount of money for each partner's own use.

- If you are experiencing severe financial issues, such as debt, bankruptcy, or fraud, get expert assistance.

Sex

Another frequent source of contention for couples, particularly those in committed partnerships, is sex. Numerous concepts, including love, closeness, pleasure, and fulfillment, may be represented via sex. Diverse imaginations, expectations, tastes, and wants may also be reflected in sexual behavior. When partners vary in their degrees of sexual desire, frequency, or quality, it may lead to conflict. When partners must handle sexual problems like adultery, dysfunction, or unhappiness, sex may also lead to arguments.

Sexual disputes often stem from underlying difficulties and wants that are connected to:

- Love: When sex is lacking or unpleasant, love and affection may be expressed and enhanced via it, or they can be missing or unsatisfied. Sex may also have an impact on a person's confidence and sense of self, particularly if there are issues or difficulties with sexual compatibility or performance. Couples may argue over how to express or accept love via sex or about how to handle disappointment or rejection during a sexual encounter.

- Intimacy: When sex is ordinary or rare, it may lead to a lack of intimacy. A person's emotions and vulnerabilities may also be shown or hidden via sex, particularly if there are anxieties or worries associated with expressing one's sexual desires and sentiments. Couples may argue over how to get past obstacles or challenges related to their sexuality, as well as how to express and comprehend one another's preferences and wants.

- Pleasure: When sex is unpleasant or dull, it may cause a loss of pleasure and delight, or it can bring about and share pleasure and happiness. Additionally, sex has the power to satisfy or exacerbate dreams and expectations, particularly when they vary or go unfulfilled between partners. Couples may argue about how to make their relationship more exciting or fulfilling or about how to deal with sexual dullness or unhappiness.

In order to address the needs and underlying difficulties that lead to sex disputes, you must:

- Instead of placing blame or shame on one another for sexual issues, be open and honest in your communication about your needs, preferences, and emotions.

- Recognize and respect each other's limits, preferences, and sexual differences; do not coerce or compel one another into having sex.

- Establish and maintain a lighthearted and upbeat sexual environment, and try out novel approaches to spice up your relationship.

- If you suffer from severe sexual issues, such as abuse, addiction, or trauma, get expert assistance.

Parenting

For couples who already have children or want to have children, parenting is another frequent source of contention. Numerous concepts, like legacy, care, and duty, may be associated with parenting. Various parenting philosophies, approaches, or standards may also be seen in parenting. Differing opinions on how to punish, educate, and nurture children may lead to arguments between spouses throughout the parenting process.

When a couple juggles their duties as parents and a relationship, parenting may sometimes lead to conflict.

Parenting disagreements often stem from underlying demands and difficulties that are connected to:

- Responsibility: When parenting is unequal or unjust, there might be a lot of responsibility and labor involved, or there may be little of either. One's identity and role may be impacted by parenting, particularly when there are adjustments or shifts in the relationships or structure of the family. Couples may argue over how to evenly divide parenting responsibilities and choices, or on who gets to do what and how much.

- Care: When parenting is inconsistent or insufficient, there may be a lack of care and attention, as well as a lot of care and attention required. Goals and values may also be influenced by parenting, particularly if they vary or clash between spouses. Couples may argue over how to promote or direct their children's growth and well-being, or how to nurture or protect them.

- Legacy: When parenting is disengaged or distant, it may either establish and maintain a legacy and a link, or it can have the opposite effect. Hopes and dreams may also be shaped by parenting, particularly if they vary or are not fulfilled between spouses. Couples may argue over how to appreciate and nurture their children's uniqueness and choices or how to carry on or maintain the customs and culture of their family.

In order to resolve parental disagreements by addressing the underlying needs and difficulties, you must:

- When discussing your parenting beliefs, objectives, and worries with your kids, be open and truthful with each other. Don't undermine or contradict one another in front of the kids.

- Recognize and value one another's parenting approaches, as well as your own and your children's, and refrain from comparing or competing with one another.

- Establish a parenting schedule that is both mutually acceptable and consistent, and divide up the responsibilities and choices evenly.

- If you are experiencing severe parenting issues, like abuse, neglect, or divorce, get expert assistance.

Chores

Another frequent source of contention for cohabiting couples is domestic chores. Numerous concepts may be represented by chores, including effort, order, and cleanliness. Different routines, expectations, or standards may also be reflected in chores. When two people are not as involved, contributing, or satisfied with the domestic chores, it might lead to conflict. Couples who must split, assign, or discuss domestic duties may also experience conflict as a result of housework.

Conflicts over tasks often stem from underlying demands and difficulties that are connected to:

- Labor: When duties are uneven or underappreciated, they might involve a lot of labor and time, or they can need little of both. The productivity and efficiency of a person may also be impacted by chores, particularly if there are delays or other distractions while doing the duties. Couples may argue over how to recognize or appreciate each other's work or who handles the majority of household responsibilities.

- Order: When duties are disorganized or untidy, they may either foster a feeling of order and organization or a lack of it. Additionally, one's standards and preferences might be reflected in their chores, particularly if they vary or are irreconcilable between couples. Organizing or maintaining their living environment, as well as respecting or adjusting to one another's preferences, may lead to arguments between couples.

- Cleanliness: When duties are unfinished or unclean, they may either guarantee a certain degree of cleanliness and hygiene or a lack thereof. The health and comfort of an individual may also be impacted by domestic chores, particularly in cases where there are hazards or issues present. Divorces may result from disagreements on how to handle or avoid domestic problems or how to keep their home clean and hygienic.

In order to address the underlying needs and concerns that cause disagreements over tasks, you must:

- Avoid nagging or whining about the duties; instead, be open and honest in your communication about your requirements, preferences, and concerns about your home.

- Recognize and respect one another's expectations, norms, and domestic practices; do not dictate or criticize one another's task assignments.

- Establish and adhere to a just and mutually agreed-upon home plan, and give each spouse specific tasks and timetables.

- If you are dealing with significant issues in your home, such as clutter, hoarding, or filth, get expert assistance.

The strategies and tips to handle each topic effectively

More about the approaches and pointers to deal with each issue skillfully, as well as how to implement them in your relationship, are covered in this section.

Money

For good reason, it's often believed that arguments over money are the most frequent source of contention in relationships. Numerous concepts, including power, security, independence, prestige, and pleasure, may be represented by money. Additionally, distinct objectives, tastes, routines, or expectations might be reflected in money. When a couple's salaries, debts, spending, saving, or investment habits diverge, money may lead to arguments. When a couple needs to make financial choices together, including planning, budgeting, or shopping, money may also lead to arguments.

In order to properly resolve financial issues, you must:

- Be open and truthful about your aspirations, financial status, and worries; do not withhold information or tell lies about them. With your partner, discuss and update your earnings, spending, debts, assets, and obligations on a regular basis. Talk about your financial objectives, both short- and long-term, and your strategy for achieving them. Talk about your concerns and annoyances with money and how they impact your connection with others.

- Avoid passing judgment or offering criticism on your partner's financial decisions. Instead, show them respect and understanding for their needs, beliefs, and financial personalities. Acknowledge that your spouse may see money differently than you do, and that this does not always mean that their viewpoint is terrible or incorrect. Try to comprehend their financial objectives as well as the ideas, feelings, and behaviors that shape them. Give them credit for their abilities and contributions to the home budget, and assist in advancing and maintaining their financial security.

- Establish and adhere to a reasonable, mutually agreed-upon budget with cooperation and flexibility. Additionally, set aside a certain amount of money for each partner's own use. Together, plan and monitor your earnings and outlays, and establish reasonable and doable financial objectives. Decide on the categories or things you will buy and how much you will save, spend, or invest. Permit each spouse to have a certain amount of money for their own needs and desires without requiring them to defend or justify their actions to the other.

- If you have major financial issues, such as debt, bankruptcy, or fraud, get expert assistance as soon as possible and responsibly. Don't wait until your financial condition is out of control or intolerable, and don't attempt to work things out on your own or keep things from your spouse. Seek guidance and support from a licensed financial advisor, counselor, or attorney, and heed their advice. Share accountability and the result with your spouse, and work together to communicate throughout the process.

Sex

Couples also often argue over sex, particularly in committed partnerships. Numerous concepts may be represented by sex, including love, closeness, pleasure, and contentment. Diverse inclinations, tastes, imaginations, and expectations may also be reflected in sexual behavior. When a couple's sexual desire, frequency, or quality differs, it may lead to conflict. Conflicts arising from sexual difficulties, such as adultery, dysfunction, or unhappiness, may also be attributed to sex.

In order to properly manage sexual tensions, you must:

- Don't point the finger or shame one another for having issues with your sex; instead, be forthright and honest about your wants, desires, and emotions. Talk to your spouse about your expectations, dreams, and wishes around sex, and hear what they have to say. Tell your partner how your sexual happiness or discontent impacts you and your relationship. Don't judge or infer anything about your partner's erotic conduct or performance, and don't get defensive or personal in response to their sexual criticism.

- Avoid pressing or forcing your partner to have sex; instead, show them respect and empathy for their limits, preferences, and sexual peculiarities. Understand that it's possible for your partner to have different sexual preferences, styles, or drives than you, and that this is not always a sign of rejection or incompatibility. Make an effort to comprehend their erotic motivations, emotions, and desires, as well as how these impact their actions. Don't coerce or persuade someone into doing anything they don't want to or feel comfortable doing; instead, respect their sexual preferences and boundaries.

- Explore new avenues to spice up your sex life and be imaginative and fun in establishing and maintaining a pleasant and exciting sexual environment. Make sexual approaches, acknowledge them, and reply with interest and vigor. Tease and flirt, make jokes, and offer praise. Experiment with various roles, situations, or sensations; try new postures, places, or toys. Enjoy yourself, surprise each other, and please each other.

- If you suffer from severe sexual issues, such as abuse, addiction, or trauma, get professional assistance as soon as possible and responsibly. Don't attempt to conceal your sexual problems from your spouse or disregard them; instead, don't try to figure things out on your own. Seek guidance and support from a licensed physician, counselor, or sex therapist, and abide by their suggestions. Throughout the process, share the conclusion and the responsibilities with your spouse and collaborate with them.

Parenting

For couples who already have children or want to have children, parenting is another frequent source of contention. Numerous concepts, like legacy, care, and duty, may be associated with parenting. Various parenting philosophies, approaches, or standards may also be seen in parenting. Differing opinions on how to punish, educate, and nurture children may lead to arguments between spouses throughout the parenting process.

When a couple juggles their duties as parents and a relationship, parenting may sometimes lead to conflict.

In order to properly manage parental disputes, you must:

- Be open and truthful with your children about your parenting beliefs, objectives, and worries. Do not undermine or contradict one another in front of the kids. Talk to your spouse about your parenting philosophies, techniques, and ideals while also listening to theirs. Talk about your parenting aspirations and difficulties, as well as how they impact you and your partner. Talk about your concerns and annoyances with parenting and how it affects both you and your kids. Don't belittle or disparage your spouse's parenting choices or methods, and don't give your kids conflicting signals.

- Avoid comparing or competing with your spouse as a parent; instead, show respect and appreciation for their parenting approaches, abilities, and shortcomings. Acknowledge that your spouse could parent differently than you do, and that this does not always mean that their method is harmful or incorrect. Make an effort to comprehend the reasons, convictions, and feelings that drive their parenting and how they affect their conduct. Recognize their abilities and contributions to the family's well-being, and assist in their further development as parents.

- Establish and adhere to a consistent, mutually agreed-upon parenting plan with cooperation and flexibility, and distribute parenting responsibilities and choices equitably. Together, identify and resolve the parenting challenges, as well as establish reasonable and doable parenting objectives. Decide together what guidelines and sanctions to follow, as well as how to teach, punish, and raise your kids. Don't let one spouse handle all the labor or decision-making when it comes to parenting; instead, divide up the duties and responsibilities.

- If you are experiencing severe parenting issues, including child abuse, neglect, or divorce, be proactive and responsible in getting expert assistance. Don't attempt to conceal your parenting challenges from your spouse or try to address them on your own. Don't dismiss or disregard them. Consult with a licensed parenting coach, counselor, or educator for guidance and support, and heed their advice. Share accountability and the result with your spouse, and work together to communicate throughout the process.

Chores

Another frequent source of contention for cohabiting couples is domestic chores. Numerous concepts may be represented by chores, including effort, order, and cleanliness. Different routines, expectations, or standards may also be reflected in chores. When two people are not as involved, contributing, or satisfied with the domestic chores, it might lead to conflict. Couples who must split, assign, or discuss domestic duties may also experience conflict as a result of housework.

In order to resolve arguments about duties, you must:

- Avoid nagging or whining about the duties, and be forthright and honest about your wants, preferences, and worries about the home. Talk to your spouse about your household's goals, objectives, and difficulties while also paying attention to theirs. Describe how you and your relationship are affected by your level of pleasure or discontent in the home. Never assume anything about your partner's performance or conduct in the home, and don't react defensively or personally to their criticism.

- Avoid managing or criticizing your partner's tasks and instead show empathy and respect for their home norms, expectations, and routines. Acknowledge that your spouse could organize or do the duties differently than you do, and

that this does not always mean that their method is terrible
or incorrect.

PART 2: THE FIVE COMMON CONFLICTS EVERY COUPLE FACES

Chapter 4: Conflict #1: The Surprise Attack

What is a surprise attack and why it happens

When one partner brings up a previously unspoken topic in an attempt to catch the other off guard and get the upper hand in negotiations, it's known as a surprise assault. One of the oldest and most deceptive bargaining strategies is the surprise assault, which may seriously harm a relationship.

Surprise attacks may be of many different kinds, including:

- Bringing up a grievance or allegation, whether recent or old, without providing prior notice or context, and then expecting a quick response or resolution.

- Exposing a secret goal or purpose that runs counter to or undermines the prior understanding or agreement between the parties.

- Threatening to break up with the other person or take extreme measures if they don't comply with particular demands.

- Presenting a false or inflated promise or claim in an attempt to coerce or shame the other partner into agreeing or complying.

- Using a friend, family member, lawyer, or deadline as a means of obtaining leverage or providing an explanation for the unexpected assault.

A surprise assault may occur for a number of reasons, including:

- Power: The attacker may have used the surprise assault to scare or influence the other partner in an effort to gain greater control or power over the relationship or circumstance.

- Fear: The attacker may employ the surprise assault as a means of self-defense or self-protection from imagined injury or loss because they feel uneasy or intimidated by the relationship or circumstances.

- Anger: The perpetrator may be angry or frustrated with the other spouse and use the unexpected assault as a means of venting or retaliating for perceived or actual wrongs.

- Greed: The attacker may use the surprise assault as a means of obtaining more or better than what they deserve or agreed to. They may have self-serving or irrational expectations or demands from the relationship or the circumstances.

- Boredom: The perpetrator may be bored and utilize the surprise assault to generate drama or excitement in the relationship or circumstance.

A surprise assault may have detrimental effects on the partnership, including:

- Distrust: The unexpected assault may cause the partners to lose faith in one another's commitment, honesty, and moral character.

- Disrespect: The partners' dignity and respect may be violated by the unexpected assault, leaving them feeling deceived, insulted, or degraded.

- Distance: The couples may feel estranged, alone, or abandoned as a result of the unexpected assault, which may also cause estrangement between them.

- Damage: A surprise assault has the potential to seriously impair a relationship and make recovery difficult or impossible.

How to deal with a surprise attack and prevent it from escalating

In order to properly respond to a surprise assault, you must:

- Remain cool under pressure and refrain from responding hastily or passionately to the unexpected assault. Inhale deeply, count to 10, or, if necessary, request a time-out.

- Ask questions and get information instead than taking the unexpected assault at face value. Inquire, seek proof, or do independent study if necessary.

- Refuse to submit to or give in to the unexpected onslaught; instead, stand up for your rights and interests. Speak your needs, wants, and preferences; furthermore, defend your relationship and yourself.

- Avoid intensifying or extending the surprise assault by engaging in compromise and negotiation. Find areas of agreement, reciprocal advantages, and win-win alternatives, then collaborate with your partner to settle the dispute.

How to use the soft start-up technique to express your feelings and needs calmly

How to use the soft start-up technique to express your feelings and needs calmly

Using the gentle start-up approach is one of the most significant skills for settling disputes in a healthy and productive manner. Renowned marital researcher and therapist Dr. John Gottman developed this strategy after discovering that the beginning of a discussion determines its outcome. He noticed that couples are more likely to get into a negative cycle of defensiveness, disdain, and obstruction when they begin their conversations with a harsh tone, criticism, or blame. Conversely, there's a greater chance that a good cycle of comprehension, empathy, and cooperation will result for couples that approach their conversations with gentleness, respect, and inquiry from the outset.

By adopting the gentle start-up approach, you may politely and gently communicate your wants and sentiments to your spouse without criticizing or blaming them. Avoiding the four toxic habits that may destroy a relationship—criticism, scorn, defensiveness, and stonewalling—can help you escape the four horsemen of the apocalypse. Inviting your spouse to listen and react positively instead of shutting down or acting badly may also be beneficial.

The following actions must be taken in order to apply the gentle start-up technique:

- Select a convenient time and location for your conversation. If you or your spouse are exhausted, hungry, stressed out, or preoccupied, don't bring up a delicate topic.

Choose a moment and location where you can both feel at ease, attentive, and serene. Respect your partner's response when you ask if they are available and eager to discuss. Decide on another time to speak if they are not ready.

- Make soft gestures and tones with your body. Avoid using abusive language, raising your voice, or making angry gestures. Talk clearly, slowly, and gently. Speak in a pleasant, kind manner, and smile when necessary. Lean forward, nod, and make eye contact. Keep your arms crossed, your eyes rolling, and your head turned away. Instead, adopt an open and carefree body language.

- Make use of "I" expressions. Avoid using "you" remarks since they might come across as accusing, critical, or accusatory. Saying something like "You never help me with the dishes" might make your spouse feel defensive and assaulted. Say something like, "I feel overwhelmed when I have to do the dishes by myself," and your spouse will be sympathetic and encouraging. When expressing your needs, wants, and preferences, use "I" statements rather than generalizations, exaggerations, or presumptions.

- Explain the circumstances, not the individual. Never categorize, belittle, or disparage your partner's characteristics or character. Saying something like, "You are so lazy and selfish," for instance, might cause your spouse to get enraged and wounded. Saying, "I feel like you don't care about me or our home when you don't do your share of the chores," might instead make your spouse feel driven and guilty. Don't use insulting language, sarcasm, or mocking while describing the particular action or circumstance that irritates you.

- Act civil and courteous. Avoid using foul, obscene, or violent words. Saying something like, "Shut up and listen to me," for instance, might cause your spouse to feel insulted and resentful. Saying, "Please listen to me out and let me finish," will instead make your spouse feel cooperative and valued. Say polite and respectful phrases like "excuse me," "please," "thank you," and "sorry." Use expressions of gratitude and admiration, such as "You are doing a great job," "I admire your skill," or "I appreciate your effort."

- Be upbeat and helpful. Avoid concentrating on the bad parts of the person or the circumstance. Saying something like, "You always mess up everything," for instance, might make your spouse feel unworthy and hopeless. Saying, "You have done many things right, but this time you made a mistake," might let your spouse feel optimistic and appreciated instead of criticizing them. Highlight the good elements of the circumstance or the individual and provide helpful criticism, recommendations, or solutions.

You may communicate your wants and sentiments to your spouse in a calm and courteous manner and raise the likelihood of a fruitful and successful discussion by using the gentle start-up approach.

Chapter 5: Conflict #2: The Emotional Tsunami

What is an emotional tsunami and why it happens

What is an emotional tsunami and why it happens

An emotional tsunami is a metaphor for an abrupt, powerful wave of emotions that might overtake your capacity for reason and self-control. Numerous things, including a painful occurrence, a demanding circumstance, a personal loss, or a problem in a relationship, might set off an emotional tsunami. Unresolved emotions that accumulate and then explode in a violent outburst may also trigger an emotional tsunami.

Your relationships, performance, and mental and physical health may all suffer greatly from an emotional tsunami. It is possible to feel useless, hopeless, or powerless during an emotional tsunami. It may also cause you to behave violently, carelessly, or impulsively. Your focus, memory, and judgment may all be affected by an emotional wave. Additionally, it may make you more susceptible to anxiety, sadness, or addiction.

Anyone may experience an emotional tsunami, regardless of their origin, age, or gender. Nonetheless, there are several things that might increase your susceptibility to an emotional tsunami, like:

- Personality: Some people are more likely to experience powerful emotions or emotional dysregulation because of their more reactive or sensitive temperament. They could also be more in need of assurance or control, or they might have a lower tolerance for stress.

- History: Individuals who have experienced trauma, abuse, or neglect in the past are at a higher risk of developing complicated PTSD or post-traumatic stress disorder (PTSD). Additionally, they can be carrying unresolved emotional scars or traumas that are quickly reactivated.

- Environment: Living in a hectic or stressful place increases a person's susceptibility to stress and possible triggers. They could also be lacking in resources or social support that might aid in their recovery or coping.

- Lifestyle: People who lead unhealthy or imbalanced lives are more likely to have emotional instability or imbalance. In addition, they could use drugs or engage in other dangerous activities that might exacerbate their emotional condition or weaken their ability to cope.

In order to stop or lessen the effects of an emotional tsunami, you must:

- Identify the warning signs and symptoms of an emotional tsunami and, if necessary, get assistance. Feeling overwhelmed, scared, or numb; racing thoughts, flashbacks, or nightmares; chest pain, palpitations, or shortness of breath; trouble sleeping, eating, or focusing; feeling alone, hopeless, or suicidal; and acting impulsively, violently, or destructively are some of the common indications and symptoms of an emotional tsunami.

- Create useful coping mechanisms and use them often. Common coping mechanisms include breathing exercises, mindfulness, or relaxation methods; physical activity, yoga, or stretching; interests, hobbies, or passions; optimism, thankfulness, or positive affirmations; social support; and counseling or therapy.

- Control your feelings and know when to let them out. Emotion management techniques include recognizing and identifying your feelings, embracing and acknowledging them, comprehending and analyzing them, controlling and releasing them, and sharing and communicating them.

You may enhance your mental and emotional well-being and use adversity as a chance for personal development by being aware of what an emotional tsunami is, why it occurs, and how to avoid or lessen its effects.

How to cope with an emotional tsunami and calm yourself down

An emotional tsunami is a metaphor for an abrupt, powerful wave of emotions that might overtake your capacity for reason and self-control. Numerous things, including a painful occurrence, a demanding circumstance, a personal loss, or a problem in a relationship, might set off an emotional tsunami. Unresolved emotions that accumulate and then explode in a violent outburst may also trigger an emotional tsunami.

Your relationships, performance, and mental and physical health may all suffer greatly from an emotional tsunami. It is possible to feel useless, hopeless, or powerless during an emotional tsunami. It may also cause you to behave violently, carelessly, or impulsively. Your focus, memory, and judgment may all be affected by an emotional wave. Additionally, it may make you more susceptible to anxiety, sadness, or addiction.

In order to calm down and manage an emotional tsunami, you must:

- Identify the warning signs and symptoms of an emotional tsunami and, if necessary, get assistance. Feeling overwhelmed, scared, or numb; racing thoughts, flashbacks, or nightmares; chest pain, palpitations, or shortness of breath; trouble sleeping, eating, or focusing; feeling alone, hopeless, or suicidal; and acting impulsively, violently, or destructively are some of the common indications and symptoms of an emotional tsunami. Do not be afraid to contact a friend, family member, or professional if you see any of these symptoms or indicators. You don't need to face this obstacle by yourself.

- Create useful coping mechanisms and use them often. Common coping mechanisms include breathing exercises, mindfulness, or relaxation methods; physical activity, yoga, or stretching; interests, hobbies, or passions; optimism, thankfulness, or positive affirmations; social support; and counseling or therapy. You may relax your body, manage your emotions, and quiet your mind with the aid of these coping mechanisms. They may also reduce emotional stress, improve your mood, and serve as a diversion from unfavorable thoughts. Make an effort to use these coping mechanisms on a daily basis or whenever you experience stress or overload.

- Control your feelings and know when to let them out. Emotion management techniques include recognizing and identifying your feelings, embracing and acknowledging them, comprehending and analyzing them, controlling and releasing them, and sharing and communicating them. You may develop awareness, understanding, and emotional self-control by using these techniques. They may also assist you in preventing emotional tsunamis by assisting you in not denying or suppressing your feelings. Alternatively, you may write, speak, or weep as healthy and productive methods to release your feelings.

How to use the repair attempts technique to reconnect and apologize

Repair efforts are words or deeds intended to keep a disagreement from becoming worse or prevent it from getting worse while also mending the relationship and mutual trust between the parties. Repair requests may be expressed verbally or nonverbally. Examples include hugging, smiling, winking, or expressing things like "I'm sorry," "I love you," or "Can we start over?" Attempts at repair may also be lighthearted or amusing, such as cracking a joke, giving praise, or making a gesture.

In order to keep a relationship pleasant and healthy, repair efforts are necessary since they can:

- Break the vicious cycle of defensiveness and negativity that may intensify a dispute.

- Even when you disagree or quarrel with your spouse, treat them with consideration.

- Without placing blame or making personal attacks on your spouse, respectfully and constructively communicate your own needs and concerns.

- Reestablish any interpersonal and emotional ties that were harmed or lost during the fight.

- Discover common ground and mutually beneficial alternatives to end the disagreement in a cooperative and collaborative manner.

Repair efforts are not always simple or successful, however. They may sometimes be overlooked, rejected, or disregarded by your spouse, particularly if there is a lot of disagreement or tension in the relationship. They may sometimes be misconstrued, misread, or abused by your spouse, particularly in cases where there is a lack of clarity in the communication or questionable motives. They may sometimes be inadequate, improper, or dishonest, particularly in cases where there is a severe disagreement or profound pain.

You must take the following actions in order to reconnect and apologize using the repair efforts technique:

- Select the ideal location and time before attempting a repair. If you or your spouse are still wounded, defensive, or furious, don't try to mend things. Hold off on talking until you are both at ease, prepared, and eager. Choose a moment and location where you can talk in privacy and without interruption. Respect your partner's response when you ask if they are receptive to hearing about your effort at mending. Decide on another time to speak if they are not ready.

- When attempting a repair, speak in a kind and honest manner. Avoid using confusing or imprecise words, as well as harsh or sarcastic tones. Talk plainly, clearly, and gently. When expressing your needs, wants, and goals, use "I" words rather than "you" ones, which might come off as condemning, accusing, or blaming. Instead of saying, "You always make me feel bad," for instance, try saying, "I feel hurt when you say that." When describing the circumstance, the issue, and the solution, use precise language and avoid making assumptions, exaggerations, or generalizations. Instead of saying, "You never listen to me," for instance, try saying, "I feel like you didn't hear what I said yesterday."

- Make an effort at mending by acting and thinking with consideration and empathy. Avoid acting in an antagonistic or violent manner or with a callous or contemptuous attitude. Even when you disagree or quarrel with your spouse, treat them with consideration. As you actively and intently listen to what they have to say, respect and affirm their viewpoint and feelings. For instance, nod and add, "I understand how you feel," rather than interrupting or rolling your eyes. Express regret and responsibility for your deeds and remarks, and offer a heartfelt apology. Saying something like, "I'm sorry for what I did or said, and I take responsibility for it," is preferable to offering justifications or excuses.

- Make an effort at mending using a constructive and good result and feedback. Avoid using harsh or unjust criticism, as well as unfavorable or damaging results. Highlight the good parts of the circumstances and your relationship while making helpful recommendations and solutions. Saying, "I appreciate what we have, and I want to make it better," is an example of how to avoid dwelling on the past or the issue. Feedback should be given and received with grace and assistance; criticism and disdain should be avoided. Say something like, "I like how you do this, and I would appreciate it if you could do that," instead of making fun of or insulting your spouse. Acknowledge and accept your partner's apologies, and express your thanks and appreciation for their mending endeavor. Say something like, "Thank you for saying or doing that, and I accept your apology," instead of ignoring them or taking them for granted.

Chapter 6: Conflict #3: The Surface Skirmish

What is a surface skirmish and why it happens

When spouses fight or dispute over little or unimportant matters, such as daily routines, personal habits, or housework, it's known as a surface skirmish. A surface-level conflict is often low-intensity, transient, and unrelated to deep or important demands or emotions. A superficial conflict may be settled quickly and simply, or it might be disregarded and forgotten.

A surface skirmish may occur for a number of causes, including:

- Stress: Due to external factors like job, family, or money, the partners may be under a lot of strain or stress and may take out their displeasure or worry on one another over trivial or unimportant issues.

- Boredom: When things get dull or boring, partners who are bored may start a fight about little matters in an attempt to liven things up or inject some energy or interest into their relationship.

- Habit: Out of habit or familiarity, the partners may have formed a pattern or routine of fighting or disagreeing about certain problems, and they may do so without giving them much consideration or significance.

- Difference: Without discovering or appreciating each other's uniqueness or variety, the partners may disagree on some topics and clash or argue over their differing tastes, viewpoints, or communication styles.

- Avoidance: The partners may utilize the surface-level conflicts as a means of avoiding or diverting attention from deeper, unresolved issues or difficulties in their relationship, rather than facing or resolving them.

A surface conflict may impact the relationship in a number of ways, including:

- Harm: If a surface conflict is persistent, severe, or disrespectful, it may be harmful to the relationship. It may lead to animosity, anger, or bitterness between the spouses, as well as undermine their mutual trust, respect, and love.

- Assistance: If a surface conflict is infrequent, minor, or productive, it may benefit or strengthen the connection. In addition to fostering humor, excitement, or variation, it may reduce relationship stress, tension, or boredom.

- Hide: If a superficial skirmish is used as a means of avoiding or running away from deeper or true concerns or problems in the relationship, it may conceal or cover such issues. It may make it difficult for the partners to express, comprehend, or find a solution for their actual requirements, wants, or worries.

In order to properly manage a surface skirmish, you must:

- Determine the origins and consequences of the surface skirmish and recognize it. Don't downplay or emphasize the surface skirmish; instead, acknowledge its presence and its significance. Regarding the nature, importance, causes, and aftermath of the surface skirmish, be truthful and practical.

- Agree on a course of action for resolving the surface conflict and any underlying or connected concerns. Don't run from or put off the conversation about the surface skirmish or its resolution, and don't try to push your viewpoint or solution on others. Regarding how and when to resolve the surface conflict, as well as any underlying issues or related issues, be helpful and accommodating.

- Discuss and compromise with your companion over the surface skirmish and any potential fixes or substitutes. Don't excuse or defend yourself, nor should you condemn or blame your spouse for the little altercation. Express your personal preferences and wants while also showing your spouse respect and empathy. Regarding the surface skirmish and its possible solutions or consequences, be upbeat and encouraging.

How to avoid a surface skirmish and address the real issue

When spouses fight or dispute over little or unimportant matters, such as daily routines, personal habits, or housework, it's known as a surface skirmish. A surface-level conflict is often low-intensity, transient, and unrelated to deep or important demands or emotions. A superficial conflict may be settled quickly and simply, or it might be disregarded and forgotten.

A surface-level disagreement, meanwhile, may also indicate a more significant or deeper issue or problem in the relationship, such as:

- Lack of communication: The partners may not be able to effectively, honestly, or politely communicate their needs, emotions, or problems due to a lack of communication skills. They could also be unable to hear, comprehend, or feel the feelings or viewpoints of one another. They could thus have misconceptions, misreadings, or presumptions that cause arguments about unimportant issues.

- Lack of intimacy: The partners may not discuss their ideas, emotions, or experiences with one another and may have little to no closeness in their relationship. Additionally, they may not express love, gratitude, or support for one another. They might thus experience feelings of alienation, loneliness, or unlove and turn to arguments about unimportant or trivial issues as a means of obtaining attention, validation, or excitement.

- Lack of trust: The partners may not appreciate, value, or honor one another's decisions, preferences, or limits, and they may have little to no trust in one another. Additionally, they could not be truthful, devoted, or committed to one another. Consequently, they can have feelings of insecurity, jealousy, or suspicion and might question, dispute, or criticize one another over unimportant or petty issues.

- Lack of contentment: It's possible that the partners don't satisfy each other's needs, wants, or expectations, which results in poor or no satisfaction in the relationship. They may not have the same values, hobbies, or ambitions. They could get irritated, dissatisfied, or bored and start arguing or complaining about unimportant things.

In order to resolve the true problem and prevent a superficial conflict, you must:

- Determine and accept the true problem, together with its origins and consequences,that underlies the surface conflict. Don't exploit the surface skirmish as a means of sidestepping or escaping the true problem, nor should you minimize or deny its presence or significance. Regarding the nature and importance of the actual problem, as well as its causes and effects, be truthful and practical.

- Agree on a plan of action for resolving the actual problem as well as any underlying or associated concerns. Avoid avoiding or delaying the conversation about or settlement of the actual problem, and do not try to push your viewpoint or solution on others. When it comes to addressing the actual problem, as well as any related issues or its core cause, be helpful and accommodating.

- Talk to your spouse about the true problem, any potential fixes, and other options. Engage in negotiation. Don't defend or excuse yourself, nor should you point the finger at your spouse for the true problem. Express your personal preferences and wants while also showing your spouse respect and empathy. Regarding the actual problem as well as any possible solutions or results, be upbeat and supportive.

How to use the X-Y-Z formula to state your complaint constructively

When one spouse is unhappy with the other's actions or mindset, it is one of the most frequent causes of conflict in a relationship. But not every complaint is made equally. While some complaints may be detrimental and destructive, others can be constructive and beneficial. It's all about how you phrase your grievance.

A constructive complaint centers on the particular conduct or circumstance that irritates you, its impact on you, and the desired change or resolution. Constructive complaints are sincere, polite, and focused on finding solutions. It facilitates efficient communication of your wants and emotions to your spouse, encouraging cooperation and listening.

A destructive complaint is one that focuses on your partner's whole attitude or character, places blame or fault on them, and then makes a demand or ultimatum of them. Destructive complaints are accusatory, forceful, and rude. It damages your partner's emotions and sense of self, and it makes them respond defensively or violently.

Using the X-Y-Z formula is one of the finest methods to express your issue in a constructive manner. Thomas Gordon, a psychologist and the author of "Parent Effectiveness Training," created this method. You may communicate your issue in a straightforward, succinct, and non-threatening manner by using the X-Y-Z formula. There are three components to it:

- X: The particular action or circumstance that irritates you.

- Y: How it affects you or how it makes you feel.

- Z: The modification or fix that you would want to see or ask for.

The X-Y-Z formula may be used in a number of circumstances, including:

- when your significant other is late for an appointment or date.

- when the person you asked to do something forgets to do it.

- when your significant other says or does anything that offends you.

- when your significant other overspends on something that you disagree with.

Here are some instances of how to formulate your complaint constructively using the X-Y-Z formula:

- I feel let down and irrelevant (Y) when you are late for our date (X). If you could either be on time or notify me ahead of time if you will be late, that would be much appreciated (Z).

- I become irritated and bitter when you don't take out the garbage as we promised (X) and (Y). Please do your portion of the housework, and let me know if you need any assistance (Z).

- I feel wounded and uncomfortable (Y) when you make fun of my choices or looks (X). I want you to support me and value my uniqueness, or you may keep your thoughts to yourself (Z).

- I feel concerned and abandoned (Y) when you spend excessive amounts of time or money on video games or shopping (X). I want you to be more balanced and responsible, or you may include me in your interests or hobbies (Z).

Chapter 7: Conflict #4: The Deadlock

What is a deadlock and why it happens

When two people come to a standstill and are unwilling or unable to go forward or make any changes, it's known as a deadlock. Numerous things may lead to a stalemate, including:

- Incompatibility: The partners may not be able to establish common ground or a workable solution because of their conflicting or irreconcilable objectives, values, or beliefs.

- Rigidity: The partners may be unable to give in or make concessions, and they may have firm or unyielding beliefs or views.

- Pride: The partners could be unable to accept or recognize their own shortcomings or faults due to their inflated or swollen egos.

- Fear: The partners may not be able to trust or take a chance on themselves or their relationship because of poor or shaky self-esteem.

- Anger: The partners could be unable to forgive or let go of their grudges or complaints due to strong or unresolved emotions.

A stalemate may have detrimental effects on the partnership, including:

- Dissatisfaction: The impasse may leave the partners feeling angry, dissatisfied, or upset as they are unable to satisfy their requirements or achieve the anticipated results.

- Disconnection: When a couple is in a stalemate, it may cause them to feel abandoned, alone, and distant from one another.

- Deterioration: The relationship may suffer and become weaker as a result of the impasse, leaving it open to outside dangers and temptations.

- Dissolution: A stalemate may ruin a relationship and make it unattractive or impossible for it to go on or become better.

In order to end or prevent a stalemate, you must:

- Acknowledge the impasse, as well as its roots and consequences. Don't minimize or downplay the impasse or its effects, and don't point the finger at or accuse your spouse of being at fault. Regarding the nature, meaning, causes, and effects of the impasse, be truthful and practical.

- Agree on a course of action to address the impasse and any underlying or related prcblems. Avoid avoiding or delaying the conversation or breaking the impasse, and don't push your viewpoint or your answer by force. Regarding how and when to resolve the impasse, as well as any underlying issues or related issues, be cooperative and adaptable.

- Discuss and work out a compromise with your spouse on the impasse and any potential fixes. Don't excuse or defend your own actions, nor should you condemn or blame your spouse for their viewpoint or actions. Express your personal preferences and wants while also showing your spouse respect and empathy. Regard the impasse, its possible solutions, and its possible results in a positive and constructive light.

How to break a deadlock and reach a compromise

While breaking a stalemate and coming to a compromise is difficult, it is doable and satisfying. It calls for both parties to have bravery, inventiveness, and patience. Here are some methods and pointers for doing that:

- **Determine the main reason for the impasse.** Sometimes the deeper, underlying need or value that is not being addressed or respected is the root of the impasse rather than the obvious problem. A standoff over money, for instance, might include issues of prestige, freedom, or security. An impasse over sex might be related to closeness, adoration, or approval. Identity, belonging, or meaning may be at issue in a religious impasse. Examine the underlying needs or values that you and your spouse are attempting to uphold or satisfy in order to determine what is really causing the dispute.

- **Make an effort to comprehend and feel the other person's perspective.** Try to listen to the other person's point of view and attempt to see the problem from their viewpoint, rather than concentrating on your own and attempting to persuade or convince the other. Pose open-ended inquiries like "What are your thoughts on this matter?" "What are your worries or anxieties?" and "What are your hopes or dreams?" Rather than passing judgment, offering criticism, or assigning blame, show empathy and affirm the other person's needs, wants, and expectations. Show respect and admiration for their values, beliefs, and preferences, as well as curiosity and interest in their ideas and views.

- **Make sure to politely and clearly state your own perspective.** It is now appropriate for you to convey your opinion once you have heard and comprehended the other person's viewpoint. To convey your needs, wants, and expectations, use "I" words such as "I feel," "I need," and "I want." Steer clear of "you" phrases that might come across as accusing, defensive, or demanding, such as "You always...", "You never...", or "You should..." Describe your stance's justifications and how they connect to your fundamental needs or beliefs. In addition to being genuine and honest, be kind and courteous. Instead of oversimplifying, generalizing, or downplaying your perspective, be realistic and detailed.

- **Look for areas of agreement and similar morals.** Once you have stated your own perspective, look for points where the other person's position and yours are similar or in accord. Seek out things that you both detest, dread, or steer clear of, as well as things that you both desire, need, or value. For instance, you could both value honesty and loyalty, or you might both desire a peaceful and joyful relationship, or you might both detest stress and conflict. Draw attention to these similarities and stress that they form the foundation of your collaboration and friendship.

Remember that you are all on the same team and that your similarities outweigh your differences.

- **Investigate original ideas and substitutes.** Try to come up with answers or alternatives that may either satisfy both of your perspectives or, at the very least, lessen the distance between them once you have established common ground and shared ideals. Strive to think outside the box and have an open mind and flexibility. Try to come up with fresh concepts or solutions that may deal with the underlying reason for the impasse as well as the fundamental requirements or ideals of both parties. Don't limit yourself to the possibilities that are already available or the status quo. At this point, instead of passing judgment on or rejecting any ideas, support and encourage one another's inventiveness and originality.

- **Make allowances and sacrifices.** Try to assess your creative ideas and alternatives once you have looked into them, and choose the one that will benefit you both. In order to satisfy the preferences or expectations of the other person, be prepared to make concessions, compromise, and give up some of your own. Consider compromise as an advantage or a gain rather than a sacrifice or a loss. Pay attention to the advantages of the compromise in the long run, such as improved closeness, harmony, and satisfaction in the partnership. Recall that making a compromise shows strength and achievement rather than weakness or failure.

- **If necessary, seek expert assistance or mediation.** Sometimes, no matter how hard you try, you can still be unable to break the impasse and come to a settlement. This might be the result of one or both parties being very obstinate, overly passionate, or overly illogical, or it could be the result of the impasse being too intricate, delicate, or entrenched. In certain situations, consulting a third-party mediator, therapist, counselor, or coach may be beneficial in getting professional assistance or mediation. They may help you and your spouse communicate, comprehend, and negotiate more effectively by offering an unbiased, impartial, and knowledgeable viewpoint on the impasse. They can also provide tools, advice, and support to help you and your partner get over the impasse and strengthen your bond.

- **Honor accomplishments and draw lessons from mistakes.** Reaching a compromise and ending a standoff is a continual process rather than an isolated occurrence. As your partnership develops and changes over time, you could run into new impasses or old ones that come back. As a result, it's critical to acknowledge your accomplishments, draw lessons from your mistakes, and use your relationships' setbacks as chances for development. Celebrate with your spouse when you are able to break an impasse and come to a compromise, and show each other thanks, admiration, and love. Instead of giving up or placing the blame on one another when you are unable to break through an impasse and come to a compromise, consider what went wrong, what can be done differently, and what lessons can be drawn from the situation.

How to use the four steps to resolve solvable problems

Not all issues result in deadlocks. Certain issues may be handled with a precise and amicable solution, which is what is meant by the term "solvable." Compared to deadlocks, solveable issues are often less sensitive, difficult, and entrenched. These could be small-minded arguments like what movie to watch or more serious matters like planning a trip.

Even Nevertheless, if handled improperly, simple issues may still lead to disputes and annoyances. It is crucial to address them in a methodical and efficient manner as a result. One method is the four-step procedure for addressing problems, which includes the following steps:

- **Define the issue.** Clearly identifying and comprehending the issue is the first step. In order to do this, the issue must be stated in precise, quantifiable words, and pertinent data and information must be gathered. The problem may be defined as follows: "We want to spend more quality time together, but we have different interests and hobbies." for instance, if the issue is that you and your spouse have different preferences on how to spend your spare time. How can we locate things to do that suit our schedules and that we both enjoy? Additionally, statistics and information on your availability, schedule, and preferences may be gathered.

- **Provide other approaches.** Creating as many potential solutions as you can via brainstorming is the second phase. This calls for creativity, openness, and the ability to weigh all available possibilities without passing judgment or rejecting any of them. We can take turns picking the activity, try new things that neither of us has done before, join a club or class that we both enjoy, plan a regular date night, compromise and do some activities separately and some together, etc. are some examples of potential solutions for the aforementioned issue. Asking your spouse or other people for advice and recommendations is another option.

- **Assess and choose a course of action.** Finding the best option that will benefit both of you is the third stage. This entails assessing the advantages and disadvantages of each choice and contrasting them with your standards and objectives. For the aforementioned challenge, some standards and objectives may be: "The solution should be enjoyable, reasonably priced, practical, and equitable." Happiness, closeness, and connection should all improve as a result of the solution. Our unique requirements and preferences should be respected in the solution. Prior to deciding on a choice, you may also experiment with or test a few options.

- **Execute the plan and monitor the outcome.** Implementing and monitoring the selected solution is the fourth and last phase. This entails organizing the solution, carrying it out, and keeping an eye on and assessing the outcomes. You may prepare and carry out the solution, for instance, by saying, "Finding a club or a class that suits our interests, budget, and schedule," if you have chosen to join a club or class that you both enjoy. registration and payment of the costs. setting up the daycare and transportation. engaging fully and showing up to the sessions. Having pleasure and relishing each other's companionship. By "asking for feedback from each other and the instructor," you may also keep an eye on and assess the outcomes. assessing our degree of pleasure and contentment. monitoring our development and advancement. Making any necessary changes or revisions.

You may solve solvable issues quickly and effectively while avoiding needless confrontations and disappointments by following the four-step procedure for problem-solving. Additionally, you may improve collaboration and communication, as well as your connection. Keep in mind that issue resolution is an ongoing process rather than a one-time occurrence. It is thus important that you are constantly prepared to address and resolve any issues that may arise in your relationship.

Chapter 8: Conflict #5: The Elephant in the Room

What is the elephant in the room and why it happens?

The phrase "elephant in the room" refers to a problem or circumstance that is evident but that people are reluctant to discuss. It is based on the notion that something as noticeable as an elephant may seem to be disregarded or overlooked in social situations because it is too awkward, contentious, or dangerous to bring up.

In partnerships, some typical instances of "elephants in the room" include:

- Infidelity includes lying, cheating, and having an affair.

- Addiction to substances like alcohol, drugs, or gambling

- Abuse includes emotional, physical, and sexual assault.

- Illness, including physical, mental, or end-stage diseases

- A loss such as a miscarriage, divorce, or death

- secrets, including bankruptcy, criminality, or a concealed history.

Elephants in the room may occur for a number of reasons, including:

- Fear may take many forms, including anxiety over the results, the responses, or the feelings that can surface from discussing the issue.

- Shame includes sentiments of shame, embarrassment, or unworthiness resulting from the issue.

- Denial is the act of not acknowledging or accepting the existence of or seriousness of an issue.

- Avoidance is the decision to ignore the issue and instead divert attention from it or concentrate on something else.

- Hope, or the conviction that the issue will disappear or be resolved on its own without assistance

- Respect is shown by actions taken to keep the other person safe or comfortable, such as avoiding discussing the issue.

Relationship-damaging effects of having elephants in the room include:

- Decreased closeness, trust, and communication in the partnership

- Relationship stress, tension, and worry have increased.

- Reduced relationship fulfillment, pleasure, and satisfaction

- Increased disputes, altercations, and altercations inside the partnership

- Reduced partners' wellbeing, confidence, and sense of self

- heightened likelihood of adultery, divorce, or separation in the partnership

As a result, it's critical to develop effective and positive coping mechanisms for handling "elephants in the room" and to use them as chances for relationship development.

How to face the elephant in the room and overcome it

It's not simple to confront and overcome the elephant in the room, but doing so is important and helpful. Both spouses must have guts, integrity, and compassion. Here are some methods and pointers for doing that:

- **Recognize the problem's existence and significance.** Admitting that there is an issue that needs to be addressed and that it is negatively impacting your relationship and general well-being is the first step. Don't act as if the issue doesn't exist, isn't that big of a worry, or will go away on its own. Rather, identify the issue and make it known that you are eager to discuss and work toward a solution. Say something like, "I realize this is a tough topic, but I think we need to talk about it." It is crucial to our pleasure and our connection. Together, I want to confront and resolve this issue.

- **Select the appropriate setting, timing, and approach for discussing the issue.** The next stage is to schedule a time, location, and mode of communication to discuss the issue. Avoid moments when you are busy, worried, or preoccupied, and instead choose a time when you and your spouse are both at ease, relaxed, and accessible. Select a location where you can be secure, comfortable, and alone; stay away from areas where you can be overheard, interrupted, or disturbed. Opt for a kind, helpful, and productive approach rather than an angry, accusing, or destructive one. Say, for instance, "Is it possible for us to discuss this tonight in our bedroom after dinner? I want to speak with you in a quiet, polite, and calm manner.

- **Discuss your own needs, wants, and emotions in relation to the issue.** Sharing your own needs, wants, and emotions about the issue and how it impacts you and your relationship is the third phase. Employ "I" statements to convey your feelings, thoughts, and expectations, such as "I feel," "I think," and "I need." Steer clear of "you" phrases that might come across as accusing, defensive, or demanding, such as "You always...", "You never...", or "You should..." In addition to being genuine and honest, be kind and courteous. Be explicit and realistic instead of generalizing, dismissing, or exaggerating your needs, emotions, or opinions. Say something like, "I feel betrayed and hurt by what you did." I believe you betrayed our vows and my confidence. You must be trustworthy and devoted to me.

- **Regarding the issue, pay attention to and comprehend the needs, emotions, and ideas of the other person.** The fourth phase is to pay attention to and comprehend what the other person is saying about the issue, how it impacts them and the relationship, and their needs. Use open-ended inquiries like "What do you think about this problem?" and "What do you need from me regarding this problem?" to get the answers you're looking for. Rather of interrupting, criticizing, or placing blame on the other person, pay attention to and affirm their needs, emotions, and opinions. Demonstrate empathy and sympathy for their circumstances while expressing curiosity and interest in their point of view. Say something like, "I understand that you feel lonely and unhappy in our relationship," as an example. I am aware that you believe I have no love or concern for you. What can I do for you to make you feel loved and cared for?

- **Seek expert assistance or support if necessary.** Sometimes, no matter how hard you try, you may not be able to confront and go over the big issue by yourself. This could occur because one or both partners are too overwhelmed, too wounded, or too resistive, or because the issue is too complicated, sensitive, or painful. Seeking professional assistance or support from a third party, such as a therapist, counselor, coach, or mediator, may be beneficial in several situations. They may help you and your relationship communicate, comprehend, and heal more effectively by offering an unbiased, impartial, and knowledgeable viewpoint on the issue. In order to help you and your partner confront the issue, conquer it, and strengthen your bond, they may also provide advice, resources, and support.

- **Collaborate to identify a solution or a course of action.** The last stage is to collaborate to identify a course of action or solution that will help you handle the issue and improve or rebuild your connection. Be open to working together, giving and receiving, and making any necessary alterations or modifications. Consider the issue as a challenge or an opportunity rather than a rivalry or a conflict. Concentrate on the advantages and long-term gains of the solution or course of action, such as improved closeness, trust, and communication in the partnership. Recall that confronting and conquering an issue is an ongoing process rather than an isolated incident. As a result, you should always be prepared to confront and resolve any issue that may arise in your relationship.

How to use the dreams within conflict technique to understand and honor each other's deepest values and goals

Occasionally, the elephant in the room is not merely a circumstance or issue but also a dream or objective that one or both partners have that runs counter to the aspirations of the other. A dream or aim is a profound and significant ambition that provides one with a feeling of fulfillment, direction, or purpose and that represents one's values, beliefs, or identity. For instance, one spouse could want to see the globe, while the other would want to put money down for retirement. Alternatively, one spouse could want to establish a family, while the other might want to focus on their work.

Couples who have opposing aspirations or objectives for their relationship may feel trapped, angry, or irritated; they may also attempt to force their beliefs on one another or avoid discussing them. This may lead to a deadlock in which neither party is prepared to give in or make concessions, which damages the relationship. But there is a way to get over the impasse and have a conversation where both parties can respect and appreciate each other's aspirations and ambitions and where the partnership may flourish. This approach, known as the dreams inside conflict method, entails the following steps:

- **Determine and share the dream or objective that motivates your stance on the dispute.** The first stage is to identify and clarify the dream or objective that guides your position in the disagreement. Since you may not be entirely aware of your own dream or objective, or you could have rejected or repressed it, this can require some introspection and meditation. Make an effort to respond to inquiries such as "What is the issue's deeper meaning or purpose for me?" and "What values or beliefs inform my position on this issue?" as well as "What hopes or fears motivate my position on this issue?" Use "I" statements to convey your dreams and goals, such as "I have a dream of..." and "I have a goal of..." Be sincere and real. Steer clear of "you" comments that come out as accusing, defensive, or demanding, such as "You don't understand..." or "You don't care about..."

- **Pay attention to and show empathy for the aspiration or objective that motivates your partner's stance on the disagreement.** The next stage is to pay attention to and show empathy for your partner's desire or objective, which is driving their position in the argument. You may not be aware of or appreciative of your partner's desire or objective, or you could have rejected it, so this might call for some empathy and inquiry. It is advisable to submit inquiries such as "What is the issue's deeper meaning or purpose for you?" "What values or beliefs inform your position on this issue?" and "What are the hopes or fears that motivate your position on this issue?" Rather than correcting, criticizing, or placing the blame on your spouse, recognize and support their aspirations. Demonstrate understanding and gratitude for their viewpoint, as well as sympathy and support for their predicament.

- **Find areas of agreement and ideals that your aspirations and ambitions have in common.** Finding points of agreement or resemblance between your aspirations is the third phase, and it should be emphasized as the cornerstone of your collaboration and partnership. Seek out things that you both detest, dread, or steer clear of, as well as things that you both desire, need, or value. For instance, you could simultaneously value security and freedom, wish to live a happy and meaningful life, or dread boredom and regret. Draw attention to these similarities and stress that they form the foundation of your working relationship. Remember that you are all on the same team and that your similarities outweigh your differences.

- **Look at original fixes and substitutes that may fulfill both of your aspirations.** The last and fourth stage is to look through your options and come up with as many solutions as you can that will either fully realize both of your aspirations or objectives, or at the very least, lessen the distance between them. Strive to think outside the box and have an open mind and flexibility. Try to come up with fresh concepts or solutions that may deal with the underlying reasons for the disagreement as well as the essential requirements or values of both parties. Don't restrict yourself to the alternatives that are already available or the status quo. At this point, instead of passing judgment on or rejecting any ideas, support and encourage one another's inventiveness and originality.

Through the use of the dreams inside conflict approach, you may confront and resolve a competing dream or desire, transforming it into a chance for personal development, education, and relationship enhancement. Along with improving intimacy, connection, and satisfaction in your relationship, you can also fortify your communication, mutual understanding, and respect. Recall that dealing with and conquering the elephant in the room is an ongoing effort rather than a one-time thing. As a result, you should always be prepared to confront and resolve any issues that may come up in your relationship.

Conclusion: The Art of Conflict

In each relationship, conflict is natural and inevitable. It represents the variety and complexity of people and is a normal and natural aspect of human connection. Diverse factors, including disparities in personality, tastes, beliefs, values, objectives, or requirements, may give birth to conflict. Additionally, a number of other things, including stress, change, or misunderstanding, might lead to conflict.

Conflict isn't always bad or detrimental, however. When handled appropriately and productively, conflict may really be useful and good. When there is conflict, there might be room for both the relationship and the person to develop, learn, and evolve. Additionally, conflict may serve as a stimulus for mutual respect, understanding, and communication. Intimacy, connection, and pleasure may also arise from conflict—in the here and now as well as in the future.

As a result, it's critical to develop your ability to handle conflict and use it to your relationship's advantage. The art of conflict is about embracing, managing, and resolving conflict rather than avoiding, concealing, or eradicating it. The art of conflict is about cooperating and producing rather than about winning, losing, or compromising. The art of conflict resolution involves listening, empathizing, and offering assistance rather than battling, disputing, or placing blame.

We've covered a number of the most prevalent and difficult conflict situations that couples encounter in this book, along with some of the most useful and workable solutions. We have also included some of the most motivational and effective narratives and illustrations of couples who have perfected the art of conflict resolution, using their disagreements as chances for development, education, and advancement.

We really hope that this book has improved your understanding of the importance and possibilities of conflict as well as your capacity to cultivate and perfect the art of conflict resolution. It is our goal that this book has motivated you to confront and resolve any dispute that may occur in your relationship and to use it as a springboard for development. With the help of this book, we hope you will be able to cultivate and preserve a joyful, close, and harmonious relationship with your spouse and reap the fruits of mastering the art of dispute.